THE POWER OF TRAVUCATION

HOW TRAVEL CAN CHANGE YOUR LIFE FOR THE BETTER!

DEVESH GOLANI

Contents

Preface

The idea of this book started with a bathtub. Yes, you read it right; it all started when I was taking a bath in the bathtub. You see, I always dreamed of having a bathtub, but I could not have it as the infrastructure of my home didn't allow me to have it installed.

However, this was one of the few times I got a great deal on this Airbnb which had this nice cosy bathtub, and of course, given my love for bathtubs, I didn't leave the chance to have a bath in it daily. But to my surprise, I realised many things which led me to write this book.

So, from the eagle's perspective, I only wanted a bathtub, but when I got one, I realised, oh, without the heater, the water is too cold, and I would need a heater to have warm water in the bathtub.

Soon enough, I realised something more, even with the heater on, there was a limited supply of hot water based on the heater's capacity, and after a few mins, it was again cold water. So I had to switch the heater on and off again for consistent warm water.

There was a huge lesson in all this for me. Most of the time, we just want something like a bathtub, luxury car, or big house, but we never think of what other factors they come with. As for the above example, I never thought it was not enough just to have a bathtub; rather, I would need a heated bathtub for a smooth experience. For a luxury car, a lot goes into maintenance and insurance, and it takes 10x time for any repairs to happen. With a big house, a lot of maintenance, cleanliness and other factors chip in.

But suppose you somehow have the experiences of these things before actually owning or having them. In that case, you will be more prepared, clear with your exact wants and needs and always have a mentality to factor in other factors and not just do wishful thinking. I call this 'Travucation'.

'Travucation' is a unique education gained over time by travelling and having different experiences. It does not need to be an international or a long journey, but a mindset to learn new things from new places we go, be it national or around the world.

Once you travel, you start to learn many different things that might have never been possible to know before. Just like my bathtub story, you might always dream of living in the Himalayas or living near a dense forest. Still, unless you actually experience it, you won't know what other factors you need to know before working towards that dream. This realisation is a unique education you learn while travelling, and you become more Travucated.

Following are the chapters that are powerful Travucation in the context of different things, from the Power of Regions to the Power of Languages to the Power of Currencies. There is so much education waiting for you in this book to empower your lives with broader thoughts and know much more about the world, which can never be taught in Academic education.

I hope you enjoy reading this book as much as I enjoyed writing it.

CHAPTER ONE

THE POWER OF EAST

While the Western world comprises South and North America, European nations, New Zealand, and Australia, the Eastern civilisation encompasses Asia and the Middle East. The attitudes and behaviours of people reflect the significant cultural contrasts between the East and the West.

If you travel the world, you will see a lot of cultural differences between East and West, which are remarkably different in almost all contexts. In this chapter, we will go through the key differences I have observed in the Eastern world, like India, Pakistan, etc.

Culture

You would have always heard the common phrase, 'Well, there is a lot of cultural difference between these two', but have you wondered what makes us so different even when we all humans have the exact needs and wants?

The East has a rich cultural heritage that has resulted in a complex and fascinating modern expression. People from the East have diverse and dynamic cultures that have evolved over time, ranging from ancient civilisations like China and India to modern city-states like Japan and Singapore. It can be challenging for Westerners to grasp the significance of tradition and respect in Eastern cultures. Authority figures and tradition are greatly valued in many Eastern cultures. This is evident in their formal forms of speech and gestures of respect when greeting and interacting with others. Extended families and communities hold a vital place in Eastern cultures.

Several Eastern cultures concentrate heavily on maintaining relationships with one's family members because of the importance of the family to Eastern values. Easterners often participate in local social clubs, religious groups, and other community organisations because they prioritise belonging to a broader community. Several aspects of Eastern culture may be traced back to the influence of religious and spiritual beliefs.

Several Asian countries attribute their distinct cultures to the long-standing impact of Buddhism, Hinduism, and other Eastern religions. Respect, tradition, family, community, and spirituality are important in the East's rich tapestry of cultural practices, which have evolved over generations.

If you travucate (educate yourself while travelling), you have the edge over everyone because you will keep learning about new cultures everywhere you go.

Education

Traditional subjects and disciplines are promoted in Eastern education, which is one of its distinguishing features. Students in the East are often expected to perform better in areas such as mathematics, science, and literature. Studying by heart and repeating lessons is also heavily emphasised. It's common to put ridiculous expectations on today's students, like having them memorise lengthy texts and figure out difficult problems with sheer willpower.

Another important aspect of Eastern education is the emphasis on respect and discipline. Students are often expected to respect their teachers and elders, and the field is vital to the educational experience. This can involve strict rules and regulations and physical punishment for misbehaviour.

Clothing

In many Eastern cultures, traditional clothing is often designed to cover the body, particularly for women. This may be motivated by cultural or religious beliefs about modesty and the importance of protecting the body. For example, in Muslim cultures, women often wear garments such as the hijab, niqab, or burka, which cover the head and body as a sign of modesty and religious piety. In Hindu cultures, traditional clothing may also cover the body, particularly for women. For example, saris and lehengas are traditional garments worn by women in India and are designed to protect the body from the shoulders to the ankles.

However, it's important to note that Eastern clothing styles and practices vary significantly across different cultures and regions. Not all Eastern cultures have the same beliefs about covering the body. Some Eastern cultures may place less emphasis on protecting the body, while others may have more relaxed standards of modesty. It's also worth noting that in many Eastern cultures, traditional clothing is often worn for special occasions or ceremonies rather than daily.

Travucation helps you see this practically everywhere you go, and you will be amazed by the world's differences in clothing.

Decision-Makers

Most countries in the East believe in traditional hierarchy and instil respect for elders and their experiences. So much so that most elders are the ones who make most decisions for the whole family. This might sound strange if you are coming from a Western background, but this is true to date for most families in most Eastern countries. The belief in this is straightforward: older people are supposed to have more experience than us. Hence, they are more eligible to decide than everyone else, depending on their perspective.

As with everything else in the world, this also has pros and cons because it leaves people very dependent on elders and decision-makers and limits their growth, but some find this useful as they don't have to think of everything on their own.

Religion/Faiths

Eastern religions are diverse spiritual traditions originating in the Eastern Hemisphere, including Asia, the Middle East, and Eastern Europe. These religions focus on spiritual enlightenment, the importance of personal spiritual practice, and the belief in a divine or higher power.

One of the most well-known Eastern religions is Buddhism, which originated in India and taught the idea of "the Middle Way" between extreme self-indulgence and self-denial. Buddhism emphasises the importance of mindfulness, living in the present moment, and reincarnation, the idea that the soul is reborn into a new body after death.

Hinduism is another major Eastern religion that originated in India. Hinduism is a complex and diverse religion that includes a wide range of beliefs and practices. Still, it is generally characterised by a belief in multiple deities, the importance of ritual and devotion, and karma, the idea that a person's actions in this life will determine their fate in future lives.

Islam is a monotheistic religion that originated in the Middle East and is based on the teachings of the prophet Muhammad. Muslims believe in one all-powerful God, Allah, and follow the instructions of the Quran, the holy book of Islam. Islam emphasises the importance of faith, prayer, and charity and encourages followers to lead a life of righteousness and obedience to God.

Other Eastern religions include Taoism, which originated in China and emphasised the importance of living in harmony with the natural world, and Sikhism. This monotheistic religion originated in India and taught the importance of social justice and equality.

Overall, eastern religions focus on personal spiritual practice and believing in a higher power or divine force. These religions offer a wide range of teachings and techniques that can help individuals find meaning and purpose in their lives, and many people find that these traditions provide a deep sense of connection to the natural world and the divine.

Sexology

Discussions of sexuality and sex are probably taboo in some Eastern cultures. Social, religious, or historical factors can influence this. As an example, in some more conservative Eastern cultures, sex and sexuality are taboo themes that shouldn't be discussed in public.

It's advisable that in these communities, people are more focused on keeping their sexual orientation and practices private and restrained.

In some Eastern cultures, discussions about sex and sexuality may also be discouraged due to the influence of religious beliefs. For example, in some Muslim cultures, sexual activity outside marriage is considered sinful, and discussions about sex and sexuality may be discouraged to maintain social and moral order. Similarly, in some Hindu cultures, premarital sex may be viewed as violating traditional cultural values. Discussions about sex and sexuality may be discouraged to preserve social norms and cultural traditions.

Ultimately, the taboos of sexology in Eastern culture are shaped by a complex combination of cultural, religious, and historical factors.

Children/Population

In Eastern countries, we see human life from a very different angle because of a complex combination of cultural, religious, and historical factors. We have belief systems that make us feel obligated to have children because we cannot take our legacy forward without them. Another common reason for having children is to have a support system when old-age problems start getting real. Unlike the West, most Eastern countries do not have any social security from the government, which leads us to believe that children are the only source of support in old age.

Another important reason in the East for having children is to have someone who will continue the business and take hold of the assets one has made throughout his life. The eastern part of the world is overpopulated because some of these reasons are strongly enforced differently on each of us.

Racism

The Eastern world uniquely faces racism compared to the West. In the West, most racism occurs based on the colour of the skin. But in the East, racism is mainly based on caste, religion, ethnicity, and financial status. Millions of people are killed in the name of religious differences, a form of racism on its own.

Many marriages in Eastern countries are dictated by caste, religion, belief systems, and financial status, not by love, respect, and understanding. It is racism because people behave differently if their faith is different, just like the colour of a human being.

Travucation of this Chapter:

The whole point of this chapter is to show how the Eastern world thinks and works on different parameters, ranging from education to belief systems. This is an education that you can see and learn when you travel through Eastern countries or look into the cultures from an Eastern perspective.

As we move forward to future chapters, you will realise how everything is different in the West and how it impacts you as a traveller when you travel to learn. To keep this book interactive, write down a few lessons you have learned in your life from Eastern culture that you like or want everyone to know. Who knows? Maybe one day you can share these with someone, and it can spark a conversation.

Write down three lessons you have learned from Eastern culture that you can share with a Westerner:

1. _______________________________________.
2. _______________________________________.
3. _______________________________________.

CHAPTER TWO

THE POWER OF WEST

This chapter focuses on the different and opposite side of our world, the Western world. Depending on the context, the Western world, also referred to as the West, can refer to various continents, countries, and states, most of the time referring to Europe, North America, and Oceania.

From my travelling to the West, I can say there is so much Travucation for the Eastern world as the West focuses on very different aspects than we do. Many things might be taboo in the Eastern world but are typical in the West. Following are some of the most exciting things I have observed in the West, making them who they are.

Culture

The traditions and beliefs that make up Western culture are a complex and diverse mixture that has been moulded through many centuries of history. The West has a rich and diverse culture that reflects its distinctive history and legacy, ranging from the ancient civilisations of Europe to the contemporary cities of America and Australia.

The focus placed by Western society on individuality and personal freedom is one of its distinguishing characteristics. Many Western nations highly value individual rights and liberties, and people are urged to think and act independently. People's interactions and communication reflect this; many Western cultures use informal forms of address and take a more laid-back approach to social interactions.

The Western culture's emphasis on education and individual success is yet another significant characteristic. Many Western nations highly value academic and professional success, and people are encouraged to follow their goals and aspirations.

The history of religion and spirituality in the West is likewise extensive, with Christianity, Judaism, and other Western religions having long histories in many Western societies. These ideas continue to play a significant role in Western society today and influence how people live their lives and perceive the world.

As a result of centuries of history, the traditions and beliefs that make up Western civilisation are complex and diverse. It is a society that respects diversity, individuality, personal freedom, education, and spirituality.

Education

The emphasis on creativity and critical thinking in Western education is distinctive. Western schools and universities highly value the arts, social sciences, and humanities, and students are urged to think critically and express themselves in original and creative ways. Learning is frequently more student-centred, encouraging children to explore new concepts, ask questions, and participate in hands-on activities.

The focus placed by Western education on individuality and personal growth is another significant feature. Students are emphasised that they should pursue their own interests, passions, and career routes. This can entail encouraging students to engage in extracurricular activities and highlighting the development of their communication, critical thinking, and emotional intelligence skills.

Personally, I was enrolled in a course that was tied to California State University, Fresno, in which my subjects were Salsa Dance, Literature writing, and International Relations. This tremendously helped me to understand the importance of different things in Western education. That case of Literature writing has helped me to contemplate my ideas in books I have published.

Clothing

Clothing trends in many Western countries frequently place a greater emphasis on comfort and individual expression. People often wear clothing that reflects their particular interests and styles in Western fashion, frequently defined by a focus on individualism and self-expression. Western clothes, for instance, can range from relaxed and informal to formal and sophisticated, depending on the setting and the wearer's preferences.

The emphasis on utility and functionality in Western clothes is another significant feature. Western clothing is frequently made with comfort and functionality in mind rather than purely for aesthetics. On the other hand, Western workwear is made to be practical and functional for workplace contexts, whilst Western athletic gear is made to support physical activity and performance.

Decision-Makers

Western cultures tend to place a greater emphasis on individualism and personal autonomy when making decisions. In many Western nations, people are urged to think independently, make independent judgments, and accept responsibility for the results of those actions. Western decision-making processes frequently feature numerous perspectives and open discussions rather than depending on one or a small number of authoritative persons to make decisions for everyone, which is mirrored in the emphasis on individualism.

The emphasis on democracy and equitable representation is another significant feature of Western decision-making. People in many Western nations have an equal voice and the ability to participate in the decision-making process, which is done through a democratic process. This can ensure that all viewpoints and interests are considered and that decisions are made with the group's overall interests in mind.

The potential for conflict and paralysis, as well as the hurdles of reaching an agreement among many perspectives and interests, are only a few of the difficulties that Western decision-making systems face. Nevertheless, Western decision-making practices are a significant part of Western culture and society and are frequently considered a way to advance freedom, autonomy, and equality.

Religion/Faiths

The term "Western religions" describes a collection of religious ideologies that have their roots in the Western hemisphere, which includes Europe, the Americas, and some regions of Africa. These faiths are distinguished by a focus on faith, adherence to the Bible or other sacred texts, and worship of a single deity.

Christianity, founded on the life and teachings of Jesus Christ and has wide different varieties, including Catholicism, Protestantism, and Orthodox Christianity, and is one of the most well-known Western faiths. Christianity stresses the idea of the Holy Trinity, composed of the Father, the Son, and the Holy Spirit, and the notion that redemption is obtained by trust in Jesus.

Another significant religion with Middle Eastern roots in the West is Judaism. Judaism is built on two principles: the significance of abiding by the laws and regulations of the Torah and the idea that there is only one God, the creator of the universe. It is the cornerstone of all Abrahamic religions, such as Christianity and Islam.

Western faiths, in general, are distinguished by a high focus on faith and adherence to sacred texts. These faiths offer a solid connection to the divine and a framework for people to develop their spiritual beliefs and discover meaning and purpose.

Sexology

Although social stigmas may still be associated with some elements of sex and sexuality, talks about sex and sexuality have recently grown more open and acceptable in Western culture. Cultural, religious, historical, and current attitudes and social standards can impact this.

Sex education is now a generally acknowledged and essential component of school curricula in Western culture. Aiming to encourage healthy sexual practices, this education strives to give people knowledge and understanding of their bodies, relationships, and sexual health.

Cultural stigmas and taboos may still be attached to specific sexual conduct, such as premarital activity, despite the growing openness and acceptability of discourse about sex and sexuality in Western culture.

Population

Cultural, economic, and individual variables frequently influence belief systems towards the population and having children in Western nations. There may be less social pressure to have children for cultural, religious, or familial reasons in many Western countries. People have more freedom and choice in having children and forming families.

Many Western cultures have experienced decreased birth rates in recent years, and there can be worries about the long-term economic and social effects of an ageing population. Some Western countries have implemented measures like tax breaks or parental leave plans to encourage couples to start families.

Ultimately, there is a wide range of ideas and attitudes on having children and beginning a family among the Western population, which is influenced by a complex interplay of cultural, economic, and personal variables. While some people could view having children as essential to leaving a legacy and guaranteeing one's future, others would put their careers, travel, or other personal ambitions ahead of having children.

Racism

Racism in Western nations is frequently rooted in a legacy of slavery and colonialism. The consequence of this has been the oppression of people of colour, particularly Black individuals and the growth of a profoundly established system of white supremacy. Various forms of racism in the West include police violence, housing discrimination, and employment discrimination.

Overall, racism is still a severe issue in Western nations and has a considerable negative influence on the lives and well-being of people of colour. To address and combat racism, individuals and institutions must take decisive action, including through advocacy, education, and changes in legislation.

Travucation of this Chapter:

A different viewpoint on the globe and its many unique cultures is provided through Western travel education. Visiting these nations, one can witness and learn about the unique history, ideologies, and customs that have shaped Western societies. The goal is to grasp the distinctions between one's own culture and those experienced when travelling, not just to acquire new knowledge and experiences. Western travel education gives a thorough and fascinating experience that fosters a deeper understanding of the globe and its people, whether through touring historical sites, tasting local food, or interacting with local communities. Write down some of the lessons you think you have learned from Western culture, or if you are from India, then maybe something you picked up from Hollywood movies/shows that you really like.

Write Down Three Lessons you have learned from Western Culture that you can share with an Easterner:

1. _______________________________________.
2. _______________________________________.
3. _______________________________________.

THE INDEPENDENT POWERS

The world is so big, and it is definitely not limited to just East and West, at least not in a cultural division. There is more to it. A lot more. There are many different countries or lands which do not follow either Eastern philosophy or Western openness. They have independent thinking or sometimes a mix of both worlds. Some countries, like North Korea, Iraq, etc., are so different from the rest of the world that they cannot be classified as Eastern or Western types of the world. The problems, beliefs, and ways of working in these countries are very different from those of the rest of the world.

Hence, I call them Independent Powers because these places hold a very different variety of education one can learn, and it is equally interesting to learn about them.

I want to mention some of the exciting countries I hope to visit once in my lifetime.

North Korea

Visiting North Korea offers a rare chance to learn about one of the world's most reclusive and secretive nations. Travel to North Korea can provide insight into the society's culture, history, and political system despite the country's strict government control over what can be seen and experienced by tourists and limited access to information.

Understanding the ruling regime and the nation's late leaders, especially Kim Il-sung and his son Kim Jong-il, is among the most important lessons to be learned from a trip to North Korea. Visitors can learn about the propaganda used to mould the views and beliefs of the North Korean people while viewing the enormous statues and portraits constructed throughout the nation.

Understanding North Korea's political structure, including its one-party rule, severe censorship and propaganda, and the military's role in daily life, is another important lesson from a trip there. Visitors can view the impressive government structures, monuments, and public squares symbolising the regime's might and authority.

Travellers can also discover more about the North Korean people's distinctive cultural practices and way of life. Visitors may see the grit and resiliency of the North Korean people, who have adjusted to the country's particular conditions and continue to uphold its cultural heritage and values despite the difficulties and challenges encountered by ordinary inhabitants.

Overall, visiting North Korea can be a challenging and unusual educational experience that can deepen understanding of one of the world's most mysterious nations. However, travel to North Korea is strictly controlled and necessitates tight cooperation with a tour company that has received approval from the government. I hope to visit North Korea once in this lifetime and experience this myself.

China

Visiting China is a once-in-a-lifetime chance to get insight into one of the world's oldest civilisations and its largest and most populated country. You may find ancient palaces, temples, state-of-the-art technology and innovation in China amid modern cities and rural villages.

Learning about China's rich cultural history is a significant takeaway from any trip to the nation. The Great Wall of China, Xian's Terracotta Warriors, and Beijing's Forbidden City all offer breathtaking examples of Chinese and Asian architecture, and they are all open to tourists. Aside from participating in local traditions and celebrations like the Chinese New Year and the Mid-Autumn Festival, visitors can also study traditional Chinese medicine, martial arts, and calligraphy.

An awareness of China's tremendous economic and social progress, especially in the last few years, is another valuable takeaway from a trip there. Shanghai, Shenzhen, and Hong Kong are all bustling metropolises that showcase China's rising economic and technological power.

Travellers to China can sample the country's food bounty and peruse its local markets' wares. They can also gain insight into the Chinese people's linguistic, religious, and cultural diversity. The Chinese people are determining their country's destiny and exerting enormous influence on the world despite the hurdles posed by censorship and political limitations.

Visiting China is an excellent way to learn about one of the world's most exciting and rapidly developing countries. Tourists may experience the history, culture, and evolution of one of the world's most influential nations in both bustling urban centres and quiet rural enclaves.

Russia

Russia is one of the world's largest and culturally wealthiest countries, and visiting it is a once-in-a-lifetime experience. There is a wide variety of things to see and do in Russia, from its crowded cities to its rural outposts.

Tourists can get a glimpse of the administration's inner workings and the enduring legacy of the Soviet era in the country's architecture and the mindset of its citizens.

Travellers to Russia can experience the country's rich cuisine and culture and learn about the Russian people's passion for literature, music, and dancing. The Russian people are famous for their warm friendliness, and it is possible to fully immerse oneself in Russian culture and art while visiting Russia.

Travelling to Russia is an excellent way to learn about one of the world's most fascinating and dynamic countries, and the trip is sure to be both enriching and gratifying. Tourists will find engaging and thought-provoking experiences in Russia, regardless of their background or field of study.

Although tourism has significantly dropped after the Russia-Ukraine war, and most of the love for Russia's tourism has vanished, there is still little hope for both countries to make peace and end the war. However, maybe in the distant future, everyone will again want to visit for better reasons.

Iraq/Afghanistan

Learning about the rich history and cultural heritage of two countries with complicated and challenging political circumstances is greatly aided through travel to Iraq and Afghanistan.

Iraq's ancient history, including its role as the birthplace of civilisation and home to some of the world's most important historical and cultural monuments like Babylon and Nineveh, is one of the most valuable lessons one can take away from a trip there. The effects of recent wars and the subsequent measures to maintain Iraq's cultural heritage are on display for visitors.

Understanding the current political and security concerns, such as the continuous conflict and instability, the impact of foreign intervention, and the efforts to reconstruct the country and its society, is another valuable takeaway from a trip to Iraq. Visitors to Iraq can experience firsthand the perseverance and tenacity of a people who have overcome enormous odds.

Similarly, visiting Afghanistan is a once-in-a-lifetime chance to educate yourself on a country that has been moulded by centuries of conflict and instability, including the ongoing fighting and the consequences of foreign intervention. Travellers to Afghanistan will be able to see firsthand how the war has affected the local population and how they are working to restore their country and civilisation.

The beautiful architecture, thriving arts sector, and distinctive traditional practices and lifestyles of Afghanistan are just a few examples of the country's rich cultural history that may be appreciated on a trip there.

Visitors can gain insight into the struggles of Afghan women and the initiatives taken to improve their status in the country.

Overall, visiting Iraq and Afghanistan is an arduous and eye-opening educational experience that can help one better understand two countries influenced by intricate and often trying political, historical, and cultural events. Note that travel to these countries is strictly controlled, necessitates close collaboration with local authorities and security professionals, and should only be attempted with a complete grasp of the security situation and the necessary safety precautions.

Travucation of this Chapter:

Some places in the world are not of a mindset of Eastern or Western philosophies but are unique. They are sometimes crucial, secretive, and weird, but that is the magic of this world. The countries mentioned above are just a few examples of unique places, but there are still many unknown places, still independent of one type of philosophy.

Some parts of the world have a particular culture and philosophy that fits differently from the Eastern or Western mould. The strangeness and mystery of these locations are part of their appeal. These countries are just a few instances; I'm sure many more have yet to be explored and have managed to preserve their unique cultures.

If you have ever been to these countries, I am sure you would have so many memories or experiences to remember, but even if you have never travelled to any of these countries, what do you think one can learn from these types of countries or cultures they follow?

Write Down Three Lessons you think one can learn from the cultures or extremism of these countries:

1. _____________________________________.
2. _____________________________________.
3. _____________________________________.

CHAPTER FOUR

THE POWER OF YOU

With all the different ways of living and going on with our lives in other parts of the world, The ultimate power lies with you and your perspective.

When one travels the world, one opens himself up to a new world of experiences and opportunities, yet one viewpoint determines how one perceives these new encounters. When people travel, they bring their own unique set of beliefs, values, and experiences from their past, all of which contribute to forming their perspective on the world around them. One can gain a diverse picture of the world through travel, rather than just a simple, one-dimensional comprehension of it, thanks to the strength of one's perspective. No two people will ever have the same experiences, contributing to the overall growth of our collective knowledge of the world and one another. It serves as a timely reminder that the point of view of each individual is significant and that by appreciating the varied viewpoints of others, we can develop a more sophisticated understanding of the world and all of the complexities it entails.

Travelling to new places allows one to engage in self-reflection and introspection, making it a powerful instrument for personal development and discovering one's identity. When people travel, they expose themselves to brand-new and one-of-a-kind experiences that have the potential to question their beliefs, views, and overall thought processes. This can assist people in broadening their perspectives and achieving greater self-awareness and comprehension of the wider world.

It is very much up to the person to decide how they want their travel experiences to go. Travellers can participate in activities aligned with their beliefs and passions, seek out meaningful interactions with members of the communities they visit, and attempt to draw significant lessons from their travel experiences. People can feel more empowered and in charge of their lives if they proactively seek out these events.

The ability to confront preconceived notions and broaden one's perspective of the wider world is another advantage that travelling offers its participants. Individuals can learn to accept diversity and widen their viewpoints by expanding their horizons by becoming acquainted with various cultures, traditions, and ways of life. This has the potential to assist people in being more tolerant, open-minded, and welcoming of other people, which can ultimately lead to a life that is more rewarding and meaningful.

The individual possesses a significant amount of ability to mould their travel experiences and gain knowledge from them. Individuals can broaden their perspectives, question their ideas, and better understand the world and themselves if they travel purposefully and seek out new and significant experiences while away.

When combined with the experiences gained via travel, the strength of one's mind can become vast. How an individual approaches their journeys can significantly impact the life lessons they take away from their experiences and the amount of personal development they can accomplish as a result of their travels.

When one travels, one has the opportunity to shape their own experiences, which is one of the ways in which the power of the mind becomes apparent. The frame of mind, attitude, and strategy a traveller adopts can considerably influence their experiences and the life lessons they take from their trips. For instance, a tourist who goes on their journey with an open and curious mind is more likely to have meaningful encounters with locals, immerse themselves in other cultures, and better understand how the world works.

Additionally, the power of the mind extends to how individuals analyse and internalise the experiences they have gained while travelling. Travellers will likely obtain more profound insights and a broader awareness of both the world and themselves if they take the time to reflect on their experiences and actively try to learn from them. This can encourage personal development and self-discovery, ultimately leading to a more satisfying and meaningful life.

In conclusion, the power of the mind is significantly increased via the experience of travel and learning. Individuals can expand their horizons, challenge their beliefs, and gain a deeper understanding of the world and themselves by travelling with an open and curious mind, reflecting on their experiences, and actively seeking to learn from them. By doing so, they can tap into the power of their minds to learn from their travels, reflect on their experiences, and actively seek to learn from them.

Travucation of this Chapter:

The world is a varied place that provides various opportunities for learning and adaptation. Yet, the result is ultimately determined by an individual's point of view and the efficacy of their learning process. Each person is responsible for their education, as innumerable teachings are waiting to be discovered in the world around us. On the other hand, a person open to learning will find no better approach than travelling to accomplish this goal. To make you realise the power of your perception, write down some of those things you always thought were correct, but with some exposure to other ideas, knowledge, etc., you realise that whatever you believed about it is not the only truth. A great typical example would be that we always thought as a child that some other community is wrong due to our parents/relatives/friend's influence, but when you grow up and make friends from that community, you realise that we cannot generalise any community/religion as wrong or right, it all boils down to individual human being.

Write Down Three perceptions you thought were always correct, but after some exposure or experience, you think otherwise:

1. ____________________________________.
2. ____________________________________.
3. ____________________________________.

CHAPTER FIVE

THE POWER OF PERMISSIONS

This chapter is very close to my heart because permissions are something significant but different based on where you are born in this world. If you were born in the land of America or Japan, you might never know the struggle of someone who was born in Iraq or Pakistan.

The world is very different to people born in other places. Permissions are nothing but the Visa, which allows you to enter the country on predetermined terms. The same allowance can be very different for people from other countries.

What is a Visa?

A visa is an official document a government grants a foreign citizen to allow them to enter and remain inside that nation's borders for a predetermined amount of time. It serves the role of a permission sheet. It states that the individual has been screened by the country of destination and is permitted to enter for a particular purpose, such as travelling, working, attending school, or receiving medical treatment.

The conditions for acquiring a visa, the types of visas available, and the length of time for which they are valid might vary from country to country. A person may be required to have a visa in order to enter a nation in certain circumstances, while in others, a visa may be obtained upon arrival at the airport.

In other words, many tourists are required to get a visa, which serves as an official stamp of approval that enables them to enter and remain in a foreign nation.

Why was The Visa started in the first place?

The issuance of travel visas was initially instituted to regulate and control foreign nationals' entry into a particular nation. It provides a method for governments to screen individuals seeking to enter their territory and determine whether they meet the admission criteria. These criteria include having a legitimate reason for travel, sufficient funds, and no history of criminal activity or immigration violations. The requirement of a travel visa allows governments to monitor and manage the flow of visitors, protect their population, maintain national security, and guarantee that foreign visitors comply with the host country's rules and regulations while there.

The Real Power of Permission Lies in Your Passport!

One measure of a passport's value is the number of countries its holder can visit without a visa. A "strong" passport is one that allows its holders visa-free or visa-on-arrival travel to a large number of countries, while a "weak" passport restricts its holders to a smaller number of countries.

The economic, political, and diplomatic ties between countries, as well as the perceived safety and security of a country, all have a role in determining the value of a passport. There is a general trend toward giving more weight to passports issued by developed nations with robust economies, stable political systems, and constructive international ties.

The number of nations ready to offer visa-free travel to nationals of countries with poorer economies, political instability, or bad human rights records tends to be smaller. Consequently, visa restrictions for passport holders are also influenced by the extent of security cooperation and information sharing between countries.

Is it really fair to determine an individual human based on their passport?

From one angle, the need for travel visas can be considered a mechanism for governments to control foreigners' access to and duration of stay in their nations, safeguarding the safety of their residents and maintaining national security.

From a different angle, the visa procedure can be perceived as burdensome and unjust, particularly for people from third-world nations, as it can be difficult and expensive to obtain a visa, and the approval process can be irrational and biased.

Personally, I believe it is something unjust because people from third world nations have an as equal right to see and explore the world as people from the first world; however, the most we can always do is comply with visa rules and wait for its results, but hopefully one day we all live in a world where the person is not determined by the place he has been born.

The issuance and grant of a visa is a privilege, not a right!

If you have applied or will apply for visas for different countries, you will see this line a lot: 'The issuance and grant of a visa is a privilege, not a right'. This is a line you will come across a lot. Because every country can approve or reject your application to enter their country. For example, as an Indian, if you want to apply for a United Kingdom visa, you must prove that you have strong ties to your country and will return. You can do this by providing endless documents like your property registrations, bank statements with enough funds, your job or business proofs, and everything that proves you will come back. Still, many Visas are declined if the Immigration officer is unconvinced.

Many people cannot reach out to their own families living abroad because of rejected Visas. The permission to go and explore any land is much more complicated as you start to travel more.

However, with these rejections, you learn many different lessons in life and understand the value of a visa or a strong passport once you get it.

Travucation of this Chapter:

Visas are an essential part of international travel and mobility. Freedom of movement is increasingly seen as a human right in today's increasingly interconnected and globalized society. However, in practice, travel visas often place limitations on this privilege. The subject of visas and the authority they grant is complicated and diverse, with far-reaching effects on individuals, communities, and nations.

Permissions' discriminating potential, however, should not be overlooked. It's possible for biases based on a visa applicant's race, ethnicity, religion, or political beliefs to creep into the visa acceptance process. This can lead to situations where some people and groups are unjustly restricted in their ability to travel and take advantage of possibilities in other nations.

Permissions, in the form of travel visas, carry with them substantial power that might affect the economy. Businesses and traders often need travel visas, and travel restrictions can slow down commerce and innovation. This may hinder the progress and growth of economies, especially in developing nations.

In conclusion, the authority of visas is a complex and diverse problem with far-reaching repercussions for individuals, communities, and nations. For national security and public safety concerns, governments must regulate and manage the admission and stay of non-citizens. However, governments must also ensure that the visa procedure is fair, transparent, and prejudice-free. This way, we can ensure that the permissions system is helping people and communities thrive rather than holding them back.

Write Down Three Experiences you had with any Visa and what advice you can give to people to tackle it. If you have never applied for a visa, even then, what do you think about this system? Write down three reasons you think this is fair or not:

1. _______________________________________.
2. _______________________________________.
3. _______________________________________.

CHAPTER SIX

THE POWER OF CULTURES

What exactly is Culture, and Does it really differ that much?

In simple terms, Culture refers to the way of life, beliefs, customs, traditions, and values a group shares. It includes things like the language we speak, the food we eat, the clothes we wear, the holidays we celebrate, the music we listen to, and the way we interact with others.

Culture shapes our identities and influences our behaviours and perspectives. It's like a giant umbrella covering how a group of people think, act, and communicate. It's passed down from generation to generation, making each society unique and different from one another.

A simple example of a cultural difference between India and some of the countries like Europe/Australia is the concept of personal space and physical touch. In many European cultures, personal space is highly valued, and people tend to maintain a certain distance between themselves and others during conversations or interactions. They may feel uncomfortable with excessive physical contact with strangers or acquaintances.

On the other hand, in India, personal space is often smaller, and physical touch is more common during conversations. People may stand closer to each other, engage in more frequent handshakes, and even greet each other with hugs or cheek kisses, depending on the region and level of familiarity. Physical touch is seen as a way to express warmth, friendliness, and respect.

Another very relatable example can be from a recent movie called 'Mrs Chatterjee vs Norway'. Based on actual events in the film, some people from Norway concluded Mrs Chatterjee to be mentally unfit just because of the cultural difference. Mrs Chatterjee in the film is shown to feed her children with her hands, put a red dot on her children's forehead and show excessive attachment towards children, which in India is completely fine. Still, in Norway, this can be considered neurotic for some. If you haven't seen this film, do check out to understand more about the cultural differences between the two countries.

How can Traveling help you see different cultures around the world?

If you travel like a traveller, I bet you will see a different side of the world everywhere you go. To see different cultures, I always encourage everyone to stay on Airbnb, visit local markets and make friends. These things can teach you so many different cultures and behaviours about people. On my recent visit to Kazakhstan, I learned that in Kazakhstan, they present a chopped goat head as a symbol of respect when they visit someone's house. This is something you can never imagine unless you explore different cultures.

Travel helps you understand and realise that anything can be a custom in another country, even if that is beyond your imagination.

Travucation of this Chapter:

One can develop a more nuanced perspective of the world by visiting new places, being fully immersed in the cultures of those places, and participating in the customs of those places.

Travelling allows one to be exposed to various cultures, one of the most significant powers of which is broadening one's perspective. People can confront their preconceived notions and views when exposed to other ways of life. They can see things from a new perspective and have a deeper appreciation for the traditions and practices of different cultures. This has the potential to lead to more tolerance and comprehension and a more tolerant attitude toward people from various backgrounds.

In addition, gaining an understanding of different cultures can be an enlightening experience. People can acquire knowledge regarding various diverse customs and beliefs, such as the composition of families, modes of communication, and religious rituals. Because it allows them to view the world differently, this can be an exceptionally enlightening experience for those who have spent their entire life in the same location. This sort of experience has the potential to result in a more profound comprehension of human nature and the myriad of distinct trajectories that people's lives can take.

In addition, new experiences and memories can be gained through exposure to different cultures when travelling. Travellers can enjoy unique and fascinating activities, such as participating in regional festivals, trying out regional cuisine, and immersing themselves in new environments. This can deepen their awareness of the world and produce memories that will remain ingrained in their minds for many years. Additionally, individuals can benefit from these experiences by growing and developing as persons, learning new skills and developing new interests.

Last but not least, travelling can also provide an opportunity to meet people from various backgrounds. People can interact with residents of the area, share their thoughts and perspectives, and cultivate connections that may last a lifetime. Travellers can broaden their understanding of the world and get insight into other cultures by conversing with members of such cultures and learning about their ways of life. This has the potential to lead to increased understanding and respect, as well as help break down barriers based on cultural traditions.

In conclusion, the strength of acquiring new cultures through travel cannot be denied. Travellers can widen their horizons, develop a more profound view of the world, experience new and exciting things, and connect with people from various backgrounds when they fully immerse themselves in the cultures of the places they visit. Learning about other parts of the world and gaining firsthand exposure to the myriad ways in which people live their lives can be immensely enriched through travel.

Write Down Three Lessons you think one can learn from exposing ourselves to new cultures :

1. _________________________________.
2. _________________________________.
3. _________________________________.

CHAPTER SEVEN

THE POWER OF CURRENCIES

If you travel the world, you will realise that every country has a different currency, which is unique. Some countries do not have any coins anymore, some countries do not value their own currency, and some countries have run out of zeros to put on notes.

The world has so much to train you about economics, understanding the basic power of trade and the power of currencies only if you wish to travel and experience the magic of it. But let's start from the beginning.

Why were currencies even invented?

By offering a standard means of transaction, currencies were developed to make it easier for individuals and businesses to engage in commerce with one another. Bartering was the standard method of exchange prior to the development of monetary systems. The act of exchanging one set of goods and services for another set of goods and services directly, without the utilisation of a standard medium of exchange, is known as bartering. However, there was no guarantee that bartering would result in a successful transaction because it depended on both people involved in the deal having desires that were identical to one another.

For instance, if one person wanted to trade things with another person, but the other person did not desire the products that were being offered, there would be no possibility of a trade taking place. This was a significant disadvantage of bartering and a primary reason why currencies were developed in the first place.

By providing a standard means of exchange that is acceptable to all parties participating in a trade, currencies assist in overcoming the restrictions that are inherent to the practice of bartering. This makes it possible for individuals and businesses to effortlessly trade goods and services with one another, regardless of either party's particular requirements or preferences.

It's likely that gold and silver were used as the first forms of currency ever created. Other precious metals may have also been used. These metals were desirable for use as currencies because of their low availability, high durability, and low barrier to entry for transactions. Paper money, backed by the government's guarantee to exchange it for a predetermined amount of gold or silver, eventually replaced precious metals as the medium of exchange for monetary systems that evolved over time.

Most currencies used today are considered fiat currencies because they are not supported by physical commodities such as gold or silver. A currency issued by a government and recognised as a valid form of payment is referred to as fiat currency. There are a variety of elements that go into determining the value of fiat currencies. These factors include the stability of the government that issues the currency, the degree of economic activity, and supply and demand for the currency.

To summarise, the primary reason for the development of currencies was the need to satisfy the demand for a universal means of exchange. They started out as valuable metals and then transitioned to paper money. These days, most currencies are fiat currencies, backed only by the government's promise that issues them. The introduction of currencies has contributed to accelerating economic growth and development by vastly improving the effectiveness of commercial transactions.

What can you learn from using different currencies in different countries?

Learning about different nations, their economies, and their cultures can be gained through the experience of travelling the world and making purchases with their respective currencies. This can be a once-in-a-lifetime chance. Using a variety of currencies can teach you a few valuable lessons, including the following:

Monetary policy: The monetary policies of different countries are distinct from one another, and using the currencies of those countries can provide insight into the robustness of their economies, the function played by their central banks, and the rate of inflation that is being experienced in those countries.

The value of a country's currency is one indicator that may be used to gauge the state of that nation's economy as a whole. For instance, nations with robust economies will typically have robust currencies, whereas those with less robust economies may have less robust currencies.

Local history and culture: Because each nation issues its own distinctive currency, examining the aesthetics of that currency can give one an idea of the country's past, as well as its present and future values.

Rates of exchange: The exchange rates between different currencies are subject to fluctuation. Using a variety of currencies allows one to gain an understanding of the fundamentals behind exchange rates as well as the ways in which these rates influence international commerce and tourism.

Financial systems: Every nation has its own financial system, and by utilising a variety of currencies, you may gain an understanding of the various payment methods, banking systems, and financial rules that are in place in various regions of the world.

When taken as a whole, the potential to improve one's understanding of the world and to get greater respect for the economic, cultural, and historical diversity that exists across the globe can be provided by utilising other currencies when travelling.

Some of the Unique things you can experience in currencies around the world:

In Vietnam and many other countries, they do not take their own currency. Instead, they prefer to take US dollars as the exchange rate is quite beneficial for all vendors.

Coins of the Australian dollar include iconic Australian animals, including the kookaburra, the echidna, and the platypus.

The Japanese Yen - The yen is one of the few currencies in the world that doesn't have a symbol of its own and is represented by the symbol "¥".

The Swiss franc is regarded as one of the world's safest currencies because of Switzerland's strong economy and impartial government.

The common loon is featured on the one-dollar coin of the Canadian dollar.

The Hong Kong Dollar - Unlike most other currencies, the value of the Hong Kong Dollar is set in reference to the US Dollar.

The Indian Rupee - The rupee is one of the world's oldest currencies, with a history dating back over 2,000 years. It is symbolised by the sign "?".

The South African Rand is the country's official currency; it replaced the pound in 1961. The topography of the country inspired the origin of its name, which translates to "mountain ridge" in Afrikaans.

The Euro - The Euro is the currency of 19 of the EU's 27 member states and the world's second most traded currency, behind only the US Dollar.

Travucation of this Chapter:

It's possible to gain new perspectives on a country's culture, economy, and politics simply by travelling throughout the world and being familiar with its many forms of currency. This may be an enlightening and eye-opening experience. For instance, you can better grasp a country's history, traditions, and values by paying attention to the denominations, designs, and ways in which people use the local currency. Furthermore, comparing the exchange rates of several currencies can provide insight into the relative purchasing power of those currencies and can shed light on the economic strengths and weaknesses of a country. Observing the ways in which people spend their money on a day-to-day basis, such as whether they prefer to pay with cash or a credit card, can also shed light on their lifestyle and the kinds of products they typically buy.

In addition, being a witness to the changes in a currency that occur as a result of political or economic events can assist you in comprehending the impact that such events have on the economy of the entire world. Your comprehension of the world can significantly improve as a result of all of these observations, which can extend your viewpoint.

Write Down Three Lessons you have learned by using different currencies. Maybe any fun facts you want to remember:

1. _______________________________________.
2. _______________________________________.
3. _______________________________________.

CHAPTER EIGHT

THE POWER OF PARITY

Do you think your friend in the USA is richer than you? Let's find out!

There is something called Purchasing Power Parity (PPP), which is an economic theory that helps us understand the relative value of currencies by comparing the prices of identical goods and services in different countries. In essence, it seeks to determine whether a specific amount of money has the same purchasing power in various parts of the world. For example, in India, bread can cost 60 INR, but in the US, it can cost $3. Now, if you see it from a layman's understanding, you will say the bread is costly in the US because it's around 250 INR, but that is not true.

In every country, the earnings are very different from other countries. A person living in the USA has a median monthly salary of $5600(Approximately 5 Lakhs per month), but a person living in India has a median monthly salary of INR 50,000.

So now, with the above information, do you realise that $3 bread is cheaper in the US than bread costing INR 60 in India?

Similarly, if you think your family or your friend in the USA is earning 5 lakhs per month and is richer than you are and you have an income of 2 lakhs, then surprisingly, you are wrong.

Per the PPP calculator, You require a salary of INR 1,15,000 in India to live a similar quality of life as you would with a salary of USD 5,000 in the United States. So, if you are earning even less than your folk in the USA, you may still be earning more than them with respect to India.

You can use PPP Salary Converter at https://www.chrislross.com/PPPConverter/

However, it's important to note that PPP is a simplified economic theory and doesn't always hold perfectly in the real world. Factors like taxes, transportation costs, and trade barriers can influence the prices of goods and services, leading to deviations from PPP. Nonetheless, PPP provides a useful framework for understanding long-term trends in currency values and price levels across countries.

Now, what does PPP have to do with you and, most importantly, with travelling?

What if I tell you that you can use this understanding of PPP and turn your life completely around? Well, back in 2017, when remote working or working from home was not at all a normal thing, I still wanted it. In the journey of finding remote work, I found a job for a US company that not only allowed me to work from anywhere in the world but also paid me $5000 per month.

This blew my mind and made me realise how amazing it is to earn in USD but spend in INR. This led me to understand that for the US, giving an employee $5000 was not a big deal because that is the median salary there; however, if I can take that salary when my spending is in India in INR, it makes a huge difference.

With that job, I started travelling around the world because I could afford to live anywhere I wanted with my income. Soon enough, I met people who were doing exact same thing. Working for a company based in the USA, Australia, and Canada and living in Bali, Vietnam and other Asian countries to use the power of parity.

I met this Australian guy in Bali who used to work remotely for an Australian company. He moved to Bali, rented a huge villa with a swimming pool, and still saved more than he had saved in Australia. Not because his salary changed or he got a huge income increase, but because he started living in a country with a weaker currency and earned in a strong currency.

Now, with the power of this information and with the right efforts to find a job in your field, think about the unlimited possibilities you can have with the growth of remote working.

How can PPP help you travel far for longer times?

Some countries like the USA, UK, and Canada have the strongest currencies in the world, and I am sure you would have seen that the people from those countries can travel in a luxury way to most of the countries they visit. If you see 5-star hotels in India, many of them have Western guests, mostly from the US, Canada, and Australia.

Similarly, some countries have weaker currencies than India. If you earn INR 1,00,000 in India, you can use PPP in places like Vietnam, Bali and some other countries and live or travel for longer times and with more luxury.

I have met several couples from the West who work remotely and use the power of PPP to stay in Asian countries for 6 months and go to the most expensive countries for another 6 months; in this way, they not just travel the world but also save enough for other things in life.

Travucation from this chapter:

Purchasing Power Parity (PPP) is a really powerful tool if you know how to make use of it. This understanding will not only allow you to travel longer but also help you understand how interestingly economics can work in your favour. This concept can make your dream of Vagabond come true easily.

There needs to be great effort to do due diligence before you actually make the long term move and it is always recommended to talk with locals along with doing PPP calculations for a better understanding.

Research and Write Down three countries where you can use the power of PPP and live a luxury life with the same income you have today:

1. ______________________________________.
2. ______________________________________.
3. ______________________________________.

THE POWER OF LANGUAGES

I have travelled to some countries where English is almost nonexistent, and it had always been terrifying before I took these trips. But Thanks to technology, I could do almost everything I wanted to do as a self-tour without any guide or travel package.

The Power of Languages is really a unique thing because, interestingly, there are over 7000 languages in the world, and most of the world can speak a maximum of two to four languages depending on where they are born and what they do for a living. Imagine how many different ways exist to say the same things to each other.

It is fascinating when you travel and see how different languages impact people differently. Do you know, scientifically, some studies have shown that people who speak different languages do indeed think differently? That is why when you speak multiple languages, you open your mind to different interpretations of the same thing. Isn't that amazing power of Languages?

How does it help to Travel, and what can you learn from different languages?

Honestly, the possibilities are endless. When you travel around the world, to countries where they speak a different language than the one you understand, you start realising how primitive human beings we can become. You begin using your hand gestures, body language, and facial expressions to convey your message to people. You start behaving like a child who has not yet learned how to speak correctly. You start decrypting your language into a simple form, using simple words and trying to explain those words with your hand gestures to get things done.

The learning is mostly inward; you start to learn about yourself more than you learn about others. When you travel frequently, you begin to understand that you cannot learn all the languages in the world before you can travel, so to adjust your brain, you start simplifying your way of communicating.

Apart from this, you realise that every person/region has its own way of speaking the same thing; there have been very similar languages but very different in some aspects. With all these experiences, you start to see the beauty of different tunes in languages and different facial expressions with specific words, and it really changes something inside you.

Does it really help if I speak a foreign language?

Imagine visiting Spain and becoming fully immersed in the local way of life. Your ability to converse with locals in Spanish may drastically increase, allowing you to build stronger relationships with them. Similarly, visiting Japan and studying the language can improve your ability to comprehend cultural nuances and forge deeper connections with locals.

Travelling and learning new languages help people develop their communication abilities as well as their understanding of other cultures. We can discover a nation's history, values, and beliefs by studying its language and customs. This can aid in broadening our viewpoint and enhancing our understanding of the diversity in our world.

The strength of languages ultimately lies in their capacity to unite people and forge deep bonds. We may lower barriers and create bridges between cultures by travelling and learning new languages.

Travucation of this Chapter:

We discover that language is a potent medium for expression and communication as we explore different nations and come into contact with many tongues. We experience firsthand how language influences our comprehension of the outside world and how we perceive it. We also discover that, despite the many language distinctions, we are all fundamentally human beings with the same needs and desires.

We learn that language is much more than just a means of communication through Travel. Our culture, history, and identity are all reflected in it. We acquire a broader perspective and an understanding of the diversity of our environment when we interact with people from various languages and cultures.

Despite these variations, we discover that everyone has the same fundamental needs, wants, and emotions. We all have feelings of happiness, sadness, love, and fear, whether we are in China, Brazil, or Germany. We all have loved ones and close friends that we value sincerely. Ultimately, everybody wants to be just happy and fulfilled in life.

Travel ultimately enables us to see past differences in language and culture to the shared human experience that unites us all. We discover that despite all of our differences, we are all connected by a common humanity that is unbound by language barriers. By embracing this common experience, we may bridge cultural gaps and promote global empathy and deeper understanding.

Write Down Three Lessons you have learned from using different languages in any situation and if that helped you in achieving any different results:

1. ____.
2. ____.
3. ____.

CHAPTER TEN

THE POWER OF CUISINES

We can all agree that there is something we all need and love to have every day! The Food. We may be divided by culture, countries and continents, but the need to have a variety of food remains constant in human beings.

When we travel, we get to know about so many different cuisines available around the world, and it not only fascinates us but also gives us so many different ideas about how food can be prepared from different things. If you travel to Europe or Central America, you will find that people almost never use any species in their food. The meat or even vegetarian dishes are prepared with the least spices possible. However, if you go to any Asian country, you will find that people there use spices in almost everything.

What do we learn from having different cuisines?

Well, if you look in a way, you might never even know what people can eat unless you travel around the world. Some cuisines or meat are banned in one country but popular in another country. So you can always learn what people eat and how they think about it. For example, eating horse meat is banned or taboo in many countries, including India, but if you travel to Kazakstan, you can get Horse steak and horse Meat burgers, and people enjoy eating them. In fact, it is a tradition in Kazakstan to sit with family over weekends and enjoy Horse meat together. This exact meat is tabooed and even banned in some countries like Brazil, Poland, Israel, and among the Romani and Jews.

If you look at India, Cow meat is banned and heavily criticised, but it's easily available and eaten in the rest of the world.

So when we travel, we realise that whatever we believe in, there are people on the other side of the world with opposite beliefs, and it is quite intriguing in its own way. When we do not travel, we think only our way of eating or only our way of thinking about certain meat is correct, but when we travel, we realise that everything is made up based on what we want to believe in.

How does having different cuisines help you learn about your own taste buds and improve your health?

People who live a routine life in the same country often have a similar variety of food even if they try to eat from restaurants. This sometimes creates fatigue for your taste buds and maybe sometimes for your health because you get almost the same proteins and nutrients every day.

However, if you travel, you become forced to eat things that are not prepared as per your taste or as per your preparation. That can be a really painful attribute for people who cannot try out new things. Everyone who travels tries different cuisines by choice or force, which helps your body adjust to new ingredients and sometimes helps you get different vitamins and proteins that you might never get in your routine food.

Something you hate in one country might be something you love in another!

To give my personal example, I always hated Oats in India (And still do), but when I travelled to Azerbaijan, I saw some flavoured Strawberry oats from a company that does not sell in India. My wife got those to experiment with. Instantly, I loved those Oats because they felt like great ice cream, and for the rest of my time in Azerbaijan, I ate Oats multiple times.

This is something amazing to learn, right? I always thought I hated Oats and I would never eat them, but to my own surprise, I loved it when I got those flavoured Oats. Now, there can be an argument that I could have tried different flavoured oats in India, and maybe I would have loved it, so what's the point of travelling in this? But we need to understand that when we travel, our mind is more open to trying new things because we have already made our mind ready that we might have to try new food as we won't get the routine food we eat at home. This opens us up to try even the same things in new flavours or in different variations.

Food Eating Habits can also reveal things about people's health in the country.

When you travel and try to have traditional meals in any country, you learn a lot about how people of that country enjoy their food and in what composition or combination they intake different cuisines. For example, if you travel to Japan or countries with a higher average lifespan, you will see a huge difference in eating habits. They would refrain from indulging in binge eating, eating spices or junk food, or eating things with better nutrition.

However, if you travel to countries with obesity problems or other common health issues, you will observe that most people are fast-paced in life and eat whatever is quickly ready, in other words, fast food. Most people would have enough time to invest in slow eating or going out of the way to make their own meals.

These differences teach you a lot about the health and mindset of people in that specific country.

Travucation of this chapter:

The cuisine of any land can teach you a lot about the people of that country in terms of what they prioritise, what they think about food, and what belief systems they have created around food, mostly deeply rooted in the history of that specific land. For example, Beef is banned in India because, in ancient history, Cow was an animal that served multiple purposes. It gave milk as a healthy drink for many, cow dung that can be used as a cooking fire, and urine, which was proven for multiple utilities.

Now, if any animal provides so many benefits, people need it to be protected at any cost, or it is a loss for the whole economy. Hence, the rules were amended to make it illegal to butcher or eat cow meat/beef.

Similarly, when you travel around the world, you will find different countries have different protection systems that were once very beneficial to them; for some, it may be sheep, a goat, or it can be a horse. Also, the most fascinating part of learning is that everyone mostly has created their own story based on religion or understanding that it is easier to explain and follow.

Write down three things you learned from having different meals that you tried for the first time in life:

1. _______________________________________.
2. _______________________________________.
3. _______________________________________.

CHAPTER ELEVEN

THE POWER OF TRANSPORT

Have you ever taken the tram? Or Ropeway? or Rode, an Electric standing scooter? Or have you experienced an open scenic train? Probably not all!

How can anyone learn from just a transport?

Well, I think there is learning everywhere you look, especially if you look at different parts of the world. For example, when I travelled to Sydney in 2008 (16 years ago from now), I saw something shocking. First and foremost, most trains were double-decker, meaning when you enter the train, half of the seating is in the upper section, and half the seating is in the lower section, giving much more space for overall seating compared to any traditional trains. Second, they had over 25 platforms with only 6-7 in use. Rest were reserved for future use.

Coming from India, where we don't have enough trains, let alone extra platforms, it was something to be shocked about. It was not just a shock but a great learning about how a country's population plays a great role in infrastructure planning.

I visited Singapore in 2010 (14 years ago from now) and saw the automatic toll deduction in Taxis for the first time ever. It was nothing less than magic for me. In India, we used to line up to pay tolls everywhere, and Singapore had already automated everything. So many examples like this can teach you a lot about new systems, etc, from merely taking regular transport outside your country.

In other words, when I came back to India from other countries, I used to see a future of what can happen in future even in India, in terms of transport and other things. This gave me an edge over other people. Whenever there were talks about Fasttag or any automated toll systems, I already knew how they worked in practice.

The world is more interconnected than we would like to think!

Suppose you look into any major businesses today, or especially startups that have grown so big. In that case, they are mostly not unique ideas but implementations of similar applications or business models that became hits in other countries.

From Ola taxi to Swiggy, these are the brainchild of ideas that were already super hit in some other countries. I am not at all saying they are exactly copy-paste or that it does not take effort to do a business, but my point is that the world is not an isolated place anymore. If there is a small business model working in some country, it can be researched, replicated, and started in other places without doing all the inventions from scratch.

When we travel, we see multiple new ideas related to transport, from easy ticketing systems to easy infrastructure for a smooth travel experience. Those ideas can be a seed for our growth once we are back in our own country. Those seeds of information can sometimes really transform into ideas that still do not exist back home.

Some of the strange yet entertaining facts related to Transport from around the World

In Singapore, new private car purchases are banned because the Singapore government does not want the roads to be congested beyond control.

Some countries have different prices for cars, some of which can be driven on weekends and some on weekdays. Vice-versa is not allowed to maintain the balance of private vehicles on the road.

Some countries like Qatar, Australia, and some parts of Europe provide completely free bus transport to their citizens so as to help control pollution and not clog the roads.

Many countries have one pass for all the public transport that can be used on water ferries, buses, trains, trams, etc., which makes life easier for people who take multiple modes of transport.

Travucation from this chapter:

When we travel around the world and use different modes of transport, we soon realise there is an abundance of things to learn and understand about our interconnected world. Some places would help you understand why Private cars are banned and some places would help you understand why more cars are needed on the road. When we travel to developed countries with robust infrastructure, we can learn what the future holds for still-developing countries. This can not only teach you something but also make you smarter by knowing which companies to invest in in the future.

Using different modes of transport like ferries, flights, and trams can also help us recognise the interconnectivity of roads and waterways and how, if required, any country can use its resources to make a great transport ecosystem.

Write your first three experiences when you tried a very different mode of transport, maybe something like a rickshaw pulled by a person, horse, etc or any Tram or tube in other countries:

1. __________________________________.
2. __________________________________.
3. __________________________________.

CHAPTER TWELVE

THE POWER OF ENVIRONMENT

Impact of our surroundings

Do you know people who live near the beach are happier than those who don't? There is a scientific reason as well. It turns out that waves from the ocean generate negative ions in the air, which are associated with increased mental energy, among other benefits. In addition, just staring at the blue water can have a peaceful effect on you, according to psychological expert Richard Shuster, PsyD, who hosts the Daily Helping Podcast. On another scientific note, researchers found that listening to ocean waves can reduce muscle tension and even heart rates, both promoting better sleep.

These are just a few facts about the impact our environment can have on us. Your individual attributes mould your behaviour, but your surroundings greatly impact it.

Difference between people who live in the city and people who live in the countryside

I am sure you would have seen a lot of differences between people who live in metro cities like Mumbai, Delhi, etc. and people who live in rural areas. The difference can be from the attitude towards money, the value of time, the value of life and the speed of doing anything. People in metro cities tend to live in a fast phase, are more career-oriented, are more money-minded and want to do much more than they can handle. In contrast, people who live in the country or rural side are much more relaxed, want to grow in a decent phase and don't bother much about doing everything in a short time.

Many may argue that this is because of education differences and that people in cities are more successful than people in rural or town areas, but then how can we generalise success for everyone in one place? Some people think the more money they have, the more successful people they are despite having any other issues in life; for some, peaceful and beautiful greenery around them with even less money is a huge success. To elaborate on this point, let me share one story that might teach you a thing or two.

There was a successful CEO of a big company, and due to his heavy stress, he went on a vacation with his family to one of the nice beachside towns to enjoy some time and relax. One day, he saw a fisherman pulling his small boat with a fishnet. Instantly, being a sharp mind, this CEO had some idea and started talking with a fisherman and asked him if he does this every day. Fisherman replied, 'Yes, I do this every day and spend my day like this'.

The CEO suggested to him a business plan where we could buy more boats on loan and hire boatmen on a commission basis. The extra money those boats bring can be used to repay the loans and eventually make him debt-free, with more income from multiple ships.

Fisherman replied, 'And then what?'

CEO further suggested, 'Then you can build a company that can buy bigger boats and go far away places to catch more fish and also catch more sea animals, that can be sold for higher profits and can earn a lot more than now

Fisherman again replied, 'And then what?'

A very confused CEO said, "Then you can enjoy some time off and spend some family time doing only what you want to do."

Fisherman smiled and said, 'That is what I am already doing, right? I do some work to keep my body active, spend good family time and relax in a hut on a nearby beach. 'This may be a temporary break for you to relax, but for me, this is the way of living'.

CEO became more confused, questioning his life choices. This is happening to most of us. We are running in the direction of more growth, more money, and more work, but if we are asked 'Define Happiness', we say living on the beach is the utmost happiness. Can you see the difference between what we want and what we do in life? No wonder more people than ever are depressed because there is a split between what we want and what everyone around us is doing or expecting us to do.

Of course, not everyone wants to stay at the beach and relax forever; some people want to embrace challenges and thrive in stressful situations, but if your happiness is not defined, you will keep running in the rat race, only to realise that there is no time left in life to do anything else.

Our mindsets have many differences, and even the same person's mindset keeps changing. Much of that credit goes to the environment people live in.

Power of Choosing the Desired Climate

With the power of Travel, you can choose to stay in different places and choose your climate/environment. With Travel, you can possess the power to be in your preferred climate whenever you wish to. If you wish to experience rain, you can find a country with a rainy season and fly there; similarly, if you don't wish to experience rain in your home country, you can fly out in the rainy season to countries that are in different weather conditions.

Whenever there are heavy rains in India, I try to fly out to countries with pleasant climates. This can only be done only if you travel and learn more about different climates in different countries.

Travucation from this Chapter:

The environment/climate and surroundings around us impact more than we would like to think, and if you learn about it, only then can you try to change it for your benefit. Changing the environment on a desired basis may not be possible for most of us. Still, if there is understanding about this, we can always know ourselves better and understand how to increase our own peace and productivity.

For example, I personally hate the summer season in India. So, in the last summer season, I went to Azerbaijan, which has a cold climate in May. I planned an entire month of work and vacation in Azerbaijan, which not only gave me the power to choose my own environment but also helped me explore a new country with a new culture. It also reduced my stress to crib about the climate, electricity downtime and other factors if I had been in India. As soon as it was normal in India, I fled back.

This is the power of the environment. I could choose and make my life a bit smoother just because Travel was possibly backed with some research about which country can be best in terms of pleasant climate.

Write down three memories/experiences you remember that went smoothly or more productively because you had the desired environment:

1. ____.
2. ____.
3. ____.

CHAPTER THIRTEEN

THE POWER OF TIMEZONES

Interesting facts about Timezones and Daylight Savings

As you probably know, every country has its own timezone, and we all follow different times based on where we live. Some countries even follow multiple timezones and daylight savings to optimize it. In the past, India's cities kept their own time zones, but a unified time zone was introduced during the colonial era to streamline the railway network, which was called the Madras time zone.

If the land of any country is huge, it is proven that multiple timezones and daylight savings help millions of dollars each year. Only a few huge countries like India and China have kept a single timezone. Let me explain how a simple half-hour shift can save India millions of rupees.

Researchers from the NIAS, Bangalore, have found that India can save about 3 billion units of electricity annually by advancing our clocks by 30 minutes. This saving amounts to almost 20 per cent of evening peaking energy use and would partly reduce the deficit we presently suffer.

The proposal of advancing IST by half an hour provides maximum energy saving during evening hours when the utilities fail to supply continuous power. Load shedding is common all over the country.

The advancement of IST by half an hour only is unlikely to alter their habits. A person waking at 7 AM and going to bed at 11 PM will continue to do so, but advanced 7 AM is unaltered at 6.30 AM when the sun is already up in most parts of the country, and 11 PM is the same as unaltered 10.30 PM. In other words, people all over India will go to bed and wake up half an hour before they presently do, and thus, their waking hours will be more aligned with the daily cycle of sunshine.

Assuming lights are kept turned on for five hours from 6 to 11 (bedtime) now will be kept on from 6.30 to 11 (bedtime), that is for four and half hours, the half-hour saving on lighting leads to an energy saving of 3 billion units of energy per year for the country.

Let's come back to The Power of Timezones.

So how can we use this interesting thing of different timezones in our travel, and what can we learn from this? So, to give a simple example, let me share a relatable experience.

Say I have a morning office call around 8 AM, and I feel too lazy to attend it as it's too early. However, If I move from IST (Indian Standard Time) to another timezone, say Singapore, as an example, that is 2 hours and 30 minutes ahead of us. In other words, if it's 8 AM in India, it is 10:30 AM in Singapore. Then, my same call would be at 10:30 AM in Singapore. No doubt, my two hours did not vanish; I still had to work as per IST timings, but then I changed my routine time to start my day by just moving countries.

This can also be a boon or a curse depending on how far you are travelling from your home country, but if you are working remotely, you might have already experienced its benefits and equally harsh drawbacks.

With travel, you can choose your timezone or adjust to a new one, which can give you many different benefits if you work or have connections with your base country on a daily basis.

More Hours are Added to your day just because of different time zones.

Recently, I took a 3-month long trip to the Balkans while working remotely for an Indian company. However, because of the timezone difference of around four and a half hours, my day there started at 5 AM and ended around 1:30 PM. This was amazing for a person like me because I still had the whole day ahead of me after my official working hours. Even if I go out to explore the city after 3 PM, I still have a good amount of hours to explore and travel without compromising my work. This added more hours to my day (Even though, technically, I lived and slept almost the same hours as India).

Travucation from this chapter:

Well, there are so many interesting things to learn from different time zones and how daylight savings works in different parts of the world. If you work remotely, you can take these concepts and make your routine by just changing time zones. Time Zone difference can be used in your favour if you plan it right.

Write down three things that you can imagine to do in a much better way if you can choose your own timezone:

1. _________________________________.
2. _________________________________.
3. _________________________________.

CHAPTER FOURTEEN

THE POWER OF FRIENDSHIPS

When you travel the world, especially solo, you realise that the world is waiting for you to be friends with. When you travel and stay in hostels and take flights, you are bound to get into other people and from those places, beautiful friendships can start, which can not just be genuine but can also help you in the long run.

I met someone in Paris who was originally from Taiwan. He was a student in Paris to be a great chef. We met in a hostel for just a couple of days, and we became really good friends. As we all do, we exchanged phone numbers and social information just in case we wanted to be in touch. Guess what? I went to Taiwan the next year, and he helped me explore it like a local. I have shared this beautiful story of friendship in length in my first book 'Around the World Under 30.'

I still have friends in countries I have never been to, but because of those friendships, I feel very confident about taking those trips whenever I want. This is what Travel does to you; this is how it makes you feel connected with people who are not only from different countries but from different mindsets and different races altogether.

How Amazing are these Travel Friendships, and How do they impact our lives?

Travel friendships are special in that they frequently develop in challenging and memorable situations. These ties may be very strong, whether it be by sharing a hostel room with total strangers, going on an adventure together, or just getting along because of a common passion for travelling.

The ability to develop close relationships with people from all around the world is one of the main advantages of travelling friendships. These linkages might be extremely beneficial in a worldwide society where understanding and empathetic behaviour towards different cultures are becoming increasingly crucial. We can develop new ideas, learn about other cultures, and remove cultural barriers by becoming friends with people from various backgrounds.

Also, while we are away from home, travel friendships can provide us with a sense of connection and belonging. When we travel, we frequently find ourselves in strange places, so having a companion by our side can be comforting. Also, travel friendships can act as a support network for us when we most need it as we manage the difficulties of Travel, such as lost luggage and linguistic obstacles.

But most significantly, making new friends while travelling can inspire and motivate you. It can be tremendously motivating to meet other travellers who are living life to the fullest. We can discover that we have more energy than ever before to try new things, take chances, and pursue our own goals.

Travel friendships are priceless. They enable us to interact with individuals from around the globe, dismantle cultural barriers, and give us a sense of belonging and inspiration. Be open to the friendships that may develop the next time you travel because they are the most fulfilling aspect of your trip.

Your travel Friends can become a reason to visit new countries!

Trust me, Travel is nothing less of an addiction where one thing leads to another, and you remain excited because it's never-ending. Sometimes because of new places, sometimes because of new people, and sometimes because you want to connect with the same people you had some connection with.

When you travel and make friends in hostels, airports, etc., you run into people from extremely different paths of life, and you start to know how different the world can be. This leads to having more curiosity about those people and forming good connections. And if connections are maintained, they become a reason to visit those countries. A lot of people don't see enough reason to spend so much money to travel to every part of the world, but if you have made any good friends, you will always see a great reason to travel and meet them again.

When I went to Amsterdam for the first time, I stayed in a hostel to celebrate the new year where. I met this guy who was a postman in Paris and was there in Amsterdam to celebrate the new year, just like me. We became good friends quickly and remained in touch. The next time I planned my Europe trip, I went to Paris to meet him and have a local tour of Paris with him. It became my reason to visit Paris again, just for a person who became my friend in the hostel.

Travel Friends teach you Detachment.

When you travel frequently or travel for weeks to months, you meet amazing people who become your friends to share your time. However, as these people are from different countries and different continents, they have to return back home, and so do you.

Sometimes, this becomes very hard because you created a great connection and friendship and shared some beautiful travel moments together, and now suddenly you realise that you may never ever meet them again, you may probably lose touch over time, and they will soon become just a memory and nothing else.

This really teaches you Detachment. It teaches you that however great people you meet, however strong connections you create, everyone is just a part of our journey, and some people might be with you for years and some for just days and eventually, you have to accept this and move on to the next adventures.

Travucation of this Chapter:

Travel friendships are something to experience at least once in a lifetime, and you will realise how powerful friendships are and how amazing it feels to have friends around the world from different countries, continents, cultures, languages, etc.

Not just this, Travel friends also teach you that no one is permanent in life. However strong the connections are, we are on our journey, and we may meet great people on the way and experience these moments from time to time.

Write Down Three Lessons you think one can learn from having cross-country or cross-culture friends:

1. ____________________________________.
2. ____________________________________.
3. ____________________________________.

CHAPTER FIFTEEN

THE POWER OF BEING WRONG

Do you think you like it when you get it all wrong?

Most of the time in our life, we cherish the times when we are right. We often want to be right, but what if I tell you there is huge power in being wrong as well?

Being right feels good and boosts our confidence in whatever we do, but being wrong gives you the sense to stay humble and keep learning. Being wrong in some knowledge, understanding, and approach forces us to revisit the situation again and leaves many lessons that we could never learn if we were always right.

A Powerful Story to Understand how important it is to be wrong as to be right!

Once upon a time, in the quaint little village of Veridale, a man named Oliver had a peculiar obsession with being right. He believed he was always right, and his stubbornness earned him a rather infamous reputation among the villagers. He would argue relentlessly, never conceding even the smallest point in a debate. This behaviour cost him many friends and strained his relationships with his family.

One sunny morning, as Oliver walked through the village square, he noticed a crowd gathered around an old, weathered sign that read, "The Wisdom of Being Wrong." It triggered his curiosity, and he couldn't resist joining the group. An elderly man, Wise Old Wilbur, stood before the sign, ready to share his wisdom with the villagers.

"My dear friends," Wise Old Wilbur began, "I have learned that it is healthy to be wrong occasionally. When we admit we are wrong, we open ourselves to learning and growing opportunities. It takes great strength to acknowledge our mistakes and even greater wisdom to embrace them as valuable lessons."

Oliver scoffed at the idea. "Being wrong is for the weak and foolish," he muttered under his breath, earning disapproving glances from the villagers around him.

Wise Old Wilbur continued, undeterred. "When we insist on being right all the time, we close ourselves off from the beauty of discovery, the joy of humility, and the richness of empathy. Through our mistakes, we gain new insights, build connections with others, and become better versions of ourselves."

Oliver couldn't help but listen, albeit begrudgingly. The words of Wise Old Wilbur planted a tiny seed of doubt in his mind.

That evening, as Oliver sat alone in his cosy cottage, he couldn't shake the thoughts of Wise Old Wilbur's wisdom. He realized that he had spent his entire life trying to prove himself right, yet he felt an emptiness. He decided to try it, to be wrong about something intentionally.

The next day, he visited the village bakery, which he had always criticized for its "inferior" bread. He approached the baker and said, "I'd like to apologize. Your bread is actually quite delicious, and I was wrong to judge it harshly."

The baker, a kind-hearted woman named Emma, was taken aback by Oliver's admission. She smiled warmly and replied, "Thank you for saying that. It means a lot to me. And remember, we can all make mistakes. It's how we grow."

Oliver felt a weight lift from his shoulders as he left the bakery. He couldn't believe how liberating it felt to admit he was wrong and see its positive impact on someone else.

Over time, Oliver opened up to others, listened to their perspectives, and even asked for advice. He found that he was learning more, deepening his relationships, and, most importantly, becoming happier.

As the years passed, Oliver became a beloved member of the village. He had transformed from the stubborn man who always had to be right into a wise man who understood the value of being wrong. He knew now that being wrong was not a weakness but a stepping stone on the path to wisdom and growth.

And so, in the village of Veridale, the story of Oliver served as a reminder that it was indeed healthy to be wrong, for in those moments of humility and self-discovery, true wisdom was found.

Being wrong can be immensely helpful to you as a Traveller!

Learning Experience: When you make mistakes or wrong decisions, you gain valuable experience. This experience becomes a guide for future journeys, helping you avoid similar errors and make more informed choices. For example, Many people book most hotels based on just price but forget to consider if the stay is very far from the town and if the commute will, in fact, cost more than they would save. But once you make these mistakes, you learn from next time.

Navigational Skills: Getting lost or taking the wrong turn can help you develop better navigational skills. It encourages you to read maps, ask for directions, and use navigation apps or tools effectively. Many places have issues with maps, and people who rely solely on technology can go crazy when the maps are inefficient. But with being wrong multiple times, you start to learn from it rather than trying to be right.

Flexibility: If you embrace being wrong, you will be more flexible and adaptable. You can change plans on the fly, switch accommodations, or adjust your itineraries when necessary, making your journeys more enjoyable and stress-free.

Problem Solving: Travel often presents unexpected challenges. When you face and overcome these challenges, they build problem-solving skills. Finding solutions can be empowering, whether it's a missed flight or a cancelled reservation.

Building Resilience: Travel can be unpredictable, and dealing with wrong turns or unforeseen setbacks can build resilience. You learn to handle adversity and bounce back from disappointments.

Embracing the potential for error while travelling allows individuals to grow, learn, and connect more profoundly with the world. It's not just about the destinations but also the journey and the lessons learned along the way.

Travucation from this chapter:

People who travel are often okay to be wrong compared to people who don't travel much. The reason is very simple, people who travel know the certainty of always being right about everything is very low and hence, they are open to improvise if the plan fails or the situation goes wrong. But people who don't travel often tend to stick to the routine, following the same plan and making it almost perfect. This gives them the sense of always being right and perfect, diminishing the understanding or humbleness of ever being wrong.

For a traveller, uncertainty is not only a reality but also something they embrace, which in return allows them to be wrong and still take many more lessons from it than trying to be right and perfect.

Write down three memories when you actually learned more by being wrong than right:

1. ____.
2. ____.
3. ____.

CHAPTER SIXTEEN

THE POWER OF DEATH

This chapter is very close to me because I am always fascinated by Death; I am constantly travelling because I realise that life is very short, and the different life experiences enrich me in ways that no other way can do. Death is something true for everyone who lives. It is not something that happens to only others, but it will happen to everyone, including you and me. This reminder itself makes me enjoy the different experiences the world has to offer.

Travel Showcases How Small We Are!

Travel is a constant reminder of our smallness in the scale of things. As we travel to new areas, we are constantly reminded that there is so much more to learn about the world outside of our own little nook of it. When you travel to different places, you realise that all your problems are not unique; they are almost the same as others. You realise how tiny space you occupy in this world and how insignificant most of your fears are.

This is a very important revelation of life, without which you will always think that life is just about you and your problems are bigger than yourself, but Travel busts this myth and brings you out of these thoughts.

Travelling reminds you of your limited time.

When you travel, you really come to know how limited time we have. Some experiences remind you that one life is not enough to see and absorb so much beauty the world has to offer.

Travel sometimes can really make us feel like we haven't seen much of life because it opens us up to so many new things, cultures, and points of view that we might not have seen in our everyday lives. When we travel outside of our comfort zone, we often find ourselves in new places and unique situations that make us question what we thought we knew and broaden our views. We might also meet new people whose beliefs, values, and ways of life are very different from our own. This can be both humbling and enlightening.

Why are we so afraid of Death? And how can travel change this?

I was reading Osho's excellent book called 'The Book of Secrets', and he says, "Those who are afraid of Death are basically afraid of life. They have not lived; that is why they are so afraid of Death. And the fear is natural. If you have not lived at all, you are bound to be afraid of Death because Death will deprive you of the opportunity to live, and you have not lived yet. So if Death comes, then when will you live? One who has lived deeply is not afraid of Death. He is fulfilled; if Death comes, he can welcome and accept it. Now, whatsoever life can give, life has given. Whatsoever can be known in life, he has known it. Now, he can move into Death easily. He would like to move into Death so that he can know something unknown, something new. In sex, in love, you are fearless. You are not fighting for something in the future; this very moment is paradise, and this very moment is eternal."

So if we truly live to our fullest, Death becomes something naturally accepted phenomenon; we are so content that the fear of Death automatically decreases. People who are afraid of Death are the same people who have never lived enough. Travelling changes this to a certain extent. When you travel, you provoke many different experiences inside you, exposing you to your inner self. You start knowing what you don't like, what you like, what you love, what type of people you never want to meet, what type of feelings you want to have and so on.

This is enriching yourself with different experiences and feelings and mostly knowing yourself to the core, and to me, that is truly living your life to the fullest because you are not limited to one aspect.

Travucation of this Chapter:

Death is something that is an inevitable part of our lives, but we often forget this and continue our lives thinking that we will have time for everything later in life, and unfortunately, that day never comes. However, when you travel, you invoke so many different experiences that you start realising how tiny a place we occupy in the world and how limited we and our time are. This brings the essential change to appreciate our time and make the most of it. That is why I personally think Travel makes you think about your limited time or Death in a good way and forces you to live your life to the fullest.

Write down three things that come to your mind when you think about Death:

1. _____________________________________.
2. _____________________________________.
3. _____________________________________.

CHAPTER SEVENTEEN

THE POWER OF KNOWING VS UNDERSTANDING

In everyday conversations with anyone, we mostly say "know" and "understand" as if they mean the same thing; however, there is a small but meaningful difference between them. Knowing is being aware of something, whereas Understanding involves the capacity to interpret and comprehend the significance of what one has learned. It is not the same thing.

Although knowing and Understanding are equally crucial, the latter carries with them an advantage that is often disregarded. When we deeply comprehend a subject, we gain new perspectives and discover hidden relationships between previously unrelated facts. Knowledge is only useful if we can put it to use in novel ways, solve issues, and come up with fresh solutions when we have a firm grasp of it.

Let's consider the gap between knowing and understanding a scientific principle. You might be able to repeat the theory from memory or apply it directly if that's all you know. Take the time to grasp the principle fully. You'll be better equipped to apply it in novel contexts, draw analogies to related scientific concepts, and perhaps even make breakthroughs in the realm of principle discovery.

The Power of Knowing & Understanding in Travel

I have met so many people who understand that it is beneficial to travel, have new experiences, and see the different things in the world to increase your knowledge and perspective. But that's that. They become limited to knowing this.

The second most important step after knowing comes understanding, and only Understanding can move you and motivate you to take action because, with knowledge, you become limited and content. Still, with Understanding, you would want to feel those experiences.

Without understanding something, the knowledge is just a piece of textual information, a memory in your head that can be recited or transferred to someone who is seeking it, but that never brings Understanding because to understand, you need to experience certain things, and only then you can relate the knowledge with Understanding.

How Travelling Can Help You from in Journey of Knowledge to Understanding

When you know something, it's not enough, but you come to know this only when you understand. It's like when you learn mathematics, it's not enough, but when that same knowledge helps you understand your taxes, you realise its importance.

When you know about travelling, about other countries, other cultures, you get excited, learn about it, and that's about it. But when you plan the travel (Even if it's pushed by someone else on you) and you experience these things, it will make you understand how amazing and life-altering these are.

With only knowledge, you have information that you can just know from others, so you also have pre-determined assumptions and a pre-determined outlook. Still, when you experience these things, you create your Understanding and your reaction to it. In this process, you also break many stereotypes.

For example, I always knew that Travelling to non-English-speaking countries like Taiwan, etc., would be very hard and it would be a problem to travel by local transport. Still, when I travelled there, I realised my knowledge was limited because, with the help of technology/maps and, a translator, everything was doable and was very smooth. This created an understanding in me that it is possible to get help from certain apps and make your travel smooth even in countries that are not English Speaking.

Knowledge can make you Angry, but Understanding makes you empathic.

A lot of times, in our life, in travel, we have some prenotion about many things, we have gathered so much information that we take that knowledge as truth, and we assume it's always right. Because of this, many times, if we don't find the facts matching our gained knowledge, we feel angry or frustrated. However, if you try to understand the whole point of it, you generate tolerance even if the facts have been changed.

For example, if you know that you will get specific meals on your flight and it has been confirmed, you have this knowledge and are bound to take this as a truth. Now, for some reason, the airline could not get your specific meal because of some integrants shortage issue.

Now, with only knowledge, you have all the right to be angry and fight over the committed meal and service, but with Understanding, you realise this can happen. However, this was not supposed to happen; now, this is what it is, and you will immediately jump to understand what other options I can have that were close to my chosen meal instead of just being angry and not enjoying any other meal. This Understanding comes immensely when you travel because you realise that in travel, no knowledge can always remain true; it is bound to keep changing.

Travucation of this Chapter:

Knowledge and Understanding are very different things, although they are considered the same. Travel helps you to realise the difference between them in a very powerful way. When you travel, a lot of knowledge has the potential to become your Understanding and that Understanding makes a lot of difference in how you start to perceive things in future. Travel teaches us a lot of things about life and our potential, but it also brings a lot of Understanding about the world and mainly about ourselves.

Write Down Three situations when you really knew something but did not understand it, and how did that impact you?

1. _________________________________.
2. _________________________________.
3. _________________________________.

CHAPTER EIGHTEEN

THE ULTIMATE POWER OF TRAVUCATION

This would be my favourite and last chapter of this book. The ultimate power of travelling is about the many different things you learn, the emotions you feel, and the understanding you gain.

These are some of the best lessons I learned after travelling to many places, meeting different people and experiencing different things. I hope you really get inspired to experience these learnings yourself one day:

Humanity is Beautiful

In a world that can often feel cold and harsh, acts of kindness remind us that there is goodness and love to be found around us. Our ability to empathise is a remarkable feature of human nature that no animal has in the world. Empathy allows us to create meaningful relationships and be firm with understanding and support.

Suppose you travel to Vietnam, Laos and some of the war zone countries. In that case, you will realise that even after everything went wrong, people have shown remarkable strength and determination, often coming together to support one another in times of need.

Humanity has come together to create art, music, and literature to express in ways words cannot. Creativity has brought the whole of humankind together, dismissing the differences we have created among ourselves in the name of race, religion, etc.

Humanity is lovely because of our kindness, empathy, resilience, inventiveness, and capacity for progress. Despite our shortcomings and imperfections, we are capable of extraordinary acts of love and compassion, creating a more beautiful and just world.

Most People In The World Are Good, And The World is Much Safer Than We Think.

Most of my friends keep asking me if I had any bad experiences while travelling or encounters with people who were bad or mean, and my answer is always NO! Surprisingly, I have never had such bad experiences with people I have met anywhere.

I think if you use your common sense, are aware of your surroundings, and leave whenever there is not a good vibe, you will mostly never face any issues. I have met numerous people in hostels, airports, flights, trains, and buses, and of course, everyone has their own way and tone of expression, but inside, no one wants to harm anyone unnecessarily.

If you follow some basic rules for travelling and respect everyone along the way, the world is beautiful, with many outstanding people who would go out of their way to help you. Most of the time, you just have to ask!

The Experiences Outside Change You Inside

Many people keep asking me or even outright calling me crazy to spend my hard-earned Money on just a few hours of flights and to do what? To see new things and meet new people for a couple of weeks? They keep saying that instead of 'Wasting' my Money on travel, why don't I save it for the future, a better car, home or lifestyle?

Well, maybe what I do is crazy for them, but if I could have just one perspective to compare everyone in the world, I would compare it with Happiness. If you are happy with whatever you do, it is not crazy anymore, even if that is possessing everything in the world or staying without anything in a forest. In the end, from my perspective, everyone is trying to find peace and Happiness.

Also, I personally believe that experiences you do really change a lot of things inside you, from your perspective about the world to different emotions which would have never come out otherwise. The best part of those experiences is that they stay with you forever; they sometimes change you forever. Last I checked, no material possession had this kind of impact on any human being that lasted forever.

Money Does Not Decide Our Happiness

It might be a cliche, but growing up, even I thought that every problem could be solved by Money; only if I had more Money would I be in a better school, a better town, a better country, and everything would be obviously better. But when I travelled around the world, I realised that in most cases, Money has nothing to do with our Happiness after a point.

There has been a scientific study to understand if Money impacts Happiness, and if it does, how much does it cost to be happy? And as per the studies, Globally, income satiation occurs at $95,000 for life evaluation and $60,000 to $75,000 for emotional well-being."

So basically, after reaching a certain point, your Money does not impact your Happiness; if you earn more than $75,000 or equivalent, your income increase does not affect your emotional well-being.

This is why most people go on grinding until they have enough Money, and once they reach the peak, they realise the answer is not more Money. They suddenly start donating it, renouncing the world, or focusing on humanitarian things.

After travelling, one realises that even poverty does not equal unhappiness; you will sometimes find people in slums who are much happier than people who stay in mansions; in that case, how can we ever say that Money is the only factor in deciding our Happiness?

Despite Everything Being So Different, We All Are Same

We all keep fighting with other races, religions, and so-called countries, but if you travel the world, you realise that this is all a man-made, stupid game of power. No individual human being hates another human being for just being born on a different part of the same earth or being born in a different colour. We all have the same emotions around the world. We laugh, we cry, we love, we crave attention, and we try to create a better life.

All paths look very different, but if you look deeper, all paths are precisely the same, only with different representations. Every human is trying to gain the same emotions of love and peace and wants to be content.

This realisation changes you completely because if you don't travel, you always think everyone is so different, or people of other places are different because they have different food, culture, religion, etc. Still, when you see the world with your own eyes, you realise we all are just different waves of one sea.

Learning is The Only Path To Being Content.

I think the whole aim of this book was to make you realise that learning can change your life and that learning can be accelerated 100 times when you travel to different places and meet different people. I think learning is a real superpower that anyone can possess from anywhere in the world, and only that superpower leads you to magical things in your life.

I believe there are two types of people in the world: one who would always find excuses not to be happy, and another who would find excuses to be happy. The main and only difference between these two types of people is perspective, the knowledge they have gained about seeing things differently.

The people who find excuses to be happy most of the time have learned a bit more than others, and that little more learning of seeing life differently changes the whole course of your life. The learnings I refer to here are not factual knowledge you gain from ugly news channels but your personal understandings after being exposed to various situations and lands.

The Ultimate Power of Travucation can only be unlocked when you travel and start experiencing your growth and perspectives. The power lies in your own hands, and you just have to unlock your way of seeing things. Then, everything you see, experience, and touch is different learning, which takes you one step closer to being happy and content. The Ultimate Power of Travucation is to realise that no matter where you are, who you are and what you have, you can be content with it and still experience the bliss.

Acknowledgement

I am profoundly grateful for the remarkable individuals who have enriched my life and played a significant role in the creation of this book. Without their support, wisdom, and encouragement, this book or the idea to share all the lessons would not have been possible.

First and foremost, I extend my deepest gratitude to the people I have encountered on my global journey. Each country and culture has gifted me with invaluable lessons, and the openness and warmth with which they welcomed me will forever hold a special place in my heart. Your stories, traditions, and perspectives have shaped the pages of this book and the person I have become. I am indebted to you all.

I would like to express my sincere appreciation to my family, **especially my wife Ekta Golani, for her unwavering support throughout this writing. Special thanks to my parents, Gordhan Golani and Alka Golani, whose belief in me and my passion for exploration has been a constant source of inspiration.** Thank you for instilling in me a love for learning and always encouraging me to follow my dreams.

Finally, I want to express my deepest gratitude to the readers of this book. Thank you for embarking on this journey with me, embracing the lessons I have shared, and allowing my experiences to resonate with you. Your curiosity and open-mindedness make the world an ever-evolving place of learning and growth.

In conclusion, the creation of this book has been a collective effort, and I am profoundly grateful to each and every person who has touched my life along the way. Your kindness, love, and support have been instrumental in shaping both my personal growth and the stories shared within these pages.

I would always be grateful if this book changed the life of even one person and helped them explore this beautiful world in a better way. I would always be happy to help with anything related to this book. You can reach me at devgolani@gmail.com

Thank you.

About The Author

Devesh Golani

Enter Caption

After realizing that most young people find travelling luxurious and unnecessarily expensive, Devesh Golani has given himself out to break this stereotype, encouraging and inspiring them to travel and explore the world. Devesh is an author, Blogger, Quality Assurance Engineer, Web Developer, and avid Traveller with a great propensity to share travelling ideas on his travel blog Wanderlust Planet.

Partly, he also drives his inspiration from travelling 59 countries (July, 2024) before age 33, something he believes every youth can accomplish.

Through this book, he has tried to share all the lessons one can learn while travelling and understanding more about other parts of the same world. He firmly believes this book will help all fellow readers dive into different things one can learn.

Currently, Devesh Golani lives in Mumbai, India. He is an avid traveller and passionate about developing websites and hacking systems. Owing to his avid readership culture, he tries to read at least 3-4 books a month.

"If you have enjoyed this book or learned anything or need help related to travel, you can reach out to him at devgolani@gmail.com | Feedback is always important for a better world!"

instagram.com/deveshgolani

Also By Devesh Golani

Do you have a dream of travelling the world?

Do you want to make it happen now while you are young enough to enjoy it?

Are you concerned that you don't quite have the right mindset to make it happen?

There are few greater pleasures in life than travel, and when you experience it for the first time, it is something that will likely stay with you forever. With travel, we open our eyes to the world around us, experience exciting new cultures, try unusual foods, meet new people and make lasting friendships. Most of us understand that travelling anywhere requires a degree of planning, but what is sometimes forgotten is that it requires a certain mindset as well.

Devesh Golani's First book, **Around The World Under 30: A Secret to Travel The World Before You Turn 30**, has been written with you in mind.

If you like this book, you will certainly love the decoding of the motivation to travel the world at a young age in my previous book.